CRAZY
ANIMAL POEMS

Written and illustrated by
MARK BARDSLEY

Text and illustrations © Mark Bardsley 2018
The moral right of the author has been asserted

First published in 2018 by Mark Bardsley
www.markbardsleyillustration.co.uk

To Ella.
Mark Bardsley

ABOUT THE AUTHOR

Mark Bardsley was born in 1963 in Essex, England and spent most of his childhood in a crumbling Shropshire manor house with his eccentric family and an exotic menagerie of animals including a grumpy pony, a scruffy Afghan hound and a very loud peacock called Sylvester.

He has been a freelance artist for many years but has also taught art, constructed strange musical instruments (he plays the harp) and managed a community theatre. His illustrations have appeared on British television (including BBC 2's Autumn Watch Unsprung) and in many books and publications.

Mark has been writing humorous poetry since he was knee high to a guinea pig and this is a collection of his funniest animal poems – each one with an accompanying coloured illustration.

At the back of this book you will find some secret pages where you can compose your own poetry.

For
My Family
And Their Animals!

'Nature teaches beasts to know their friends.'
William Shakespeare
(Coriolanus)

CONTENTS

BEASTLY BUSINESS

It's a beastly business
Keeping a pet,
Cleaning up cat mess,
Involving a vet.

It's a ghastly nightmare
Scraping up sick,
Scrubbing an armchair,
Tweezing a tick.

Why do we keep them?
Why do we do it?
A beast is for life,
You cannot undo it!

Look at those eye balls
Gazing at you,
Sad and devoted –
Well, what can you do?

You can't turn your back
On a desperate creature,
You're stuck with it now
As a permanent feature.

It's a beastly business,
There's nothing else to it
And you had the choice –
Just admit it;

YOU BLEW IT!

EMBARRASSING BERTIE

Our dog is an odd sort of nondescript chap,
We call him embarrassing Bertie.
Folk generally don't want him up on their lap
'Cos his breath stinks and often he's dirty!

Our dog is the sort of dog nobody loves,
He goes in the worst kind of places.
He's best handled carefully with gardening gloves
And a hose is required in some cases.

Our dog loves us dearly, of that we are sure
And our friends numbered upwards of thirty
But now they don't come to our house anymore,
They object to embarrassing Bertie!

SPOTTY

Spotty drives me potty,
He is a dotty dog
But not dots as in spotty
(He is not a spotty dog.)

Spotty is a Scotty
And blacker than a pot.
Someone forgot that spots are not
What Spotty dog has got!

GUINEA POO

Guinea pig, my guinea pig,
Oh guinea tell me do,
Why is it that a perfect shape
Is made by guinea poo?

Most poos are soft and squishy
And random in their form
But yours are perfect every time,
Is that the guinea norm?

I cannot keep my poo as neat
However hard I try.
It always comes out such a mess,
I really wonder why?

But guinea pig, oh guinea pig,
You have the perfect poo;
A nicely formed torpedo shape,
I wish I could be you!

POOP!

I like to have my faithful doggie
Trotting by my side,
We wander 'neath the open sky
And scan horizons wide.

But there's one thing that spoils it all
When we walk round our loop;
It's when my doggie squats and does
A massive pile of poop!

I know it should not linger there,
On others it's not fair
But scraping sticky poo
From grass is more than I can bear!

It's why I'm so reluctant when
My Mum says, walk the brute.
She says he will not need to poop
Then PLOP! There stands a beaut'!

ANIMAL HOUSE

Clive the monkey glares at me
Whenever I walk past.
I hope his flimsy cage stays shut
Because Clive can move fast.

He flicks his eyebrows up and down
And bares his yellow teeth.
Another monkey lives upstairs;
He's smaller, he's called Keith.

You see, my friend collects these beasts,
I don't know where he gets them.
His house is full of animals,
They run wild, he just lets them!

He kept a panther in the bathroom,
Then, just as I feared,
One day I went to see my friend
And he had disappeared!

SCARY CAT

We have a very scary cat,
We often wonder where she's at!
She'll growl and hiss and curse and spit –
She seemed so lovely when a kit!

All other cats we'd met were cuties –
Pretty, purring, perfect beauties.
We must have some dreadful jinx
To get stuck with this vicious minx!

She nips our hands and scuffs our faces,
Flees from us to hiding places,
Picks fights with our other pets.
She's made us bitter with regrets.

We'd rather have a vampire bat
Than something scary like our cat.
The vet confirmed our greatest fears –
She's healthy and could live for years!

15

PONIES

The ponies were frisky that we rode upon,
Galloping galloping galloping on.
'Don't cry, you'll be safe' (they went like a bomb)
Galloping galloping galloping on.

We trusted our steeds with kids to be kind,
Galloping galloping galloping on.
Our parents were waving, we left them behind,
Galloping galloping galloping on.

We shouted and screamed but they were too keen,
Galloping galloping galloping on.
Revved up and running like racing machines,
Galloping hammering rocketing on.

We reached a big ditch and swerved at the edge,
Galloping rattling clattering on.
We flew through the air and went over a hedge,
Wailing and sailing and spinning along.

Wedged in the willows, weeping and white,
Tangling dangling trying to hang on.
Those mischievous ponies were nowhere in sight,
Galloping galloping galloping …..

GONE!

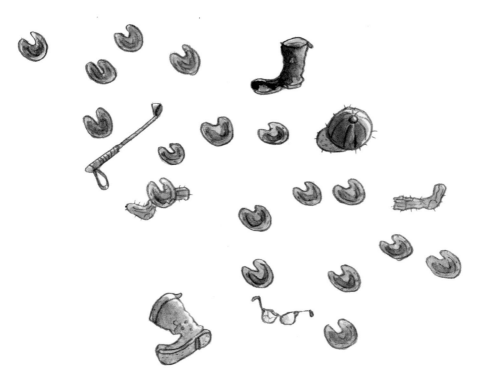

TINY CHAMELEON

I had a small chameleon,
He was a tiny thing,
So handy as a fly catcher
When out his tongue would fling!

But being rather teeny
Made him very hard to see,
Especially when his colour changed
To match our tweed settee.

He did not know the danger
He was putting himself in,
For no one in our household
Is particularly thin.

As bums landed on cushions
Up into the air he'd bounce.
He'd almost hit the ceiling
As he barely weighed an ounce.

One day my Aunty took a seat –
One cushion for each cheek.
Chameleon was trapped beneath,
I heard his feeble squeak.

But being very tiny
Proved to be his saving grace;
The gaps in bums and cushions are
To him a roomy place!

BABY OWL

Baby owl
Why do you sit
Alone upon your stump?
I'm worried that when foxes prowl
They'll eat you,
Fluffy lump!
But,
Baby owl
Knows Mummy's near
And watching from a tree.
She's waiting for the stars to shine
And then she'll bring your tea.

SQUIRRELS

Where do squirrels bury their nuts
And how do they find them, I wonder?
Do they locate them immediately
Or into them randomly blunder?

And when they so wantonly steal all my fruit
(It's a wipe-out, it's not just a trickle)
Do they run a small factory down in the woods
Where my damsons are made into pickle?

Do they run a small shop in an old hollow tree?
If they do then it couldn't be minter,
For all those that hibernate surely go there
To stock up on jam for the winter.

Do Ratty and Moley and Badger pop in
For shopping and chats with a neighbour?
If it's true I must find out and go there myself
To gather the fruits of my labour!

I THINK SHE LIKES ME MUMMY!

'I think she likes me Mummy,'
I said, clutching a kitten.
My face was only slightly scratched,
My thumbs had not been bitten.

'CAN I keep her, Mummy?
She's grinning, see her teeth?
Her claws come out to cuddle me
When I stroke her underneath.'

'I do SO like her Mummy!
My love is very real.
My fringe will soon grow back
And all my bleeding wounds will heal.'

'PLEASE let's keep her Mummy,
You know it all makes sense
And can you buy some armour
And a small electric fence?'

MICRO PIG

My micro pig is getting too big,
They assured me he'd stay fairly small.
That's my understanding but he is expanding,
He's battered a hole in the wall.

A mini they told me – a macro they sold me,
A gigantic dustbin on trotters.
He's a feral wild boar, I can't take any more.
I've been swindled by swine selling rotters!

I'm anxious with worry, my garden is slurry,
I cannot just give him the boot.
He's chewed up my chairs, eaten holes in the stairs,
I'm stuck with the ravenous brute!

I'm not against larger mammalians,
I've time for them in the right setting
But a micro pig's not like the thing that I've got,
He's a giant I wouldn't mind betting!

TARANTULA

I love my pet tarantula,
I love her hairy legs.
I pat her with a spatula
And feed her hard boiled eggs.

I love my pet tarantula,
I love her, yes I do.
I love the way that people scream
When she hides in the loo!

MY BUDGIE WON'T BUDGE!

My budgie is lovely, a chirpy wee bird,
She twitters and whistles the best tunes I've heard
But she squawked like a hawk in a terrible rage
When her head got jammed through the bars of her cage.

I teased and used tweezers, I smeared her with grease.
Her ear splitting screams were disturbing the peace!
I pulled on her tail and I pulled on her toes
But she screeched like an elephant blowing its nose!

I had to do something; I had to act quick.
The sounds of her agony made me feel sick!
So I dashed to the vets' – Messers Routledge and Rudge.
I burst in and shouted 'my budgie won't budge!'

Messers Routledge and Rudge, having promptly been paid,
Sent a nice young man round with an old hack saw blade.
My fears were unfounded, my bird had got free!
She was sat on her perch calmly nibbling her knee!

I rushed to my budgie; I rushed to her quick,
My budgie had budged her self, what a mean trick!
I felt rather foolish at this crucial stage,
So I shoved her head back through the bars of the cage.

LITTLE TINY BABY VOLE.

Little, tiny baby vole,
You whiz out from your hidey hole.
Your beady eyes can barely see
The towering giant that is me!

I stoop, I scoop you in my hand,
I lift you high above the land.
You squeak and wriggle in alarm
But I could never do you harm.

You see, you are so very cute
And though you dread the brown owl's hoot,
You brave the moon's ascending light
And scurry restlessly all night.

A DOGGIE BIT ME!

A doggie bit me on the hand!
I really cannot understand
Why, when he looked so cute and kind,
He savaged me like bacon rind.

His eyes were brown and soft and sweet,
Why did he chew me just like meat?
I wanted him to be my chum
And then he bit me on the bum!

I seem to be the one he dreads,
He's torn my trouser leg to shreds.
I only went to pat his head
But now I know he wants me dead!

KILLER CUCKOO.

I found a cuckoo plump and round,
Just sitting there upon the ground.
I can't confess that I like you,
I've heard about the things you do.

I know you mistreat baby birds!
Now, you and I, we must have words.
You cannot carry on this way –
Your greed will catch you out one day.

You soon outgrew your tiny nest
And now are huge and cannot rest.
You might be munched up by a fox
Or captured in a cardboard box.

You sit there plump and bold as brass,
Your staring eyes like yellow glass.
I don't know how your Mum and Dad
Put up with you, so big and bad!

While stuffing you with tasty flies,
Do they not view you with surprise?
They seem to love you like their own
But would they if the truth were known?

Beneath your nest their children strewn –
You'd better migrate pretty soon!

MY MUMMY FEEDS ME VEGETABLES!

My Mummy feeds me vegetables,
She says they're very healthy
But I can feed them to the dog
If he and I are stealthy.

For growth she gives me vitamins
But I can't get them down
And so I chuck them to our pooch –
The largest one in town!

My Mummy cooks me spinach,
She says it's good for muscle
And now our dog is like a horse –
He's only a Jack Russell!

A BAT IN MY BEDROOM

A bat in my bedroom's a guest I revere,
Though others give vent to loud shouting and fear.
How mean and ungrateful the people who moan are!
The bat will avoid them –
He's fitted with sonar!

THE FALSE WIDOW

There was a false widow, she led me astray –
I was lured by her web of deceit.
She sat in my window pane all the long day
Waiting for something to eat.

This false widow spun and she made a fine lace
By the light of the wintry moon.
I drew close but she pounced on me, biting my face
And my head swelled up like a balloon!

POODLE DOODLE

A poodle is oodles of doodles,
Some scribble that nibbles and dribbles.
The poodle whose food'll be noodles
Will not be a poodle who quibbles.

If a poodle has trouble with bubbles
Or hobbles when covered with bobbles.
If he gobbles his food and then wobbles
Then his nibbles are probably nobbled!

PIRATE PARROT!

Our parrot is quite odd, I think he was a pirate's bird.
The things he does all make it plain to me.
He shouts out, 'Aaaaargh! Pieces of eight,'
And other pirate words.
He sways as if he's sailing on the sea.

He gets over excited when a cork pops from a bottle
And shouts out rather rude things to my Mum!
He bobs about just like an engine piston at full throttle
And bellows, 'Get the grog boys! Where's the Rum?'

I tested him by putting chocolate pennies in his cage;
He dug a hole and buried them in seed!
I rigged a jolly roger on a stick beside his perch;
He hoisted it – what more proof did I need?

I went back to the pet shop and I said, 'Excuse me there,
My parrot is a most peculiar bird!'
The pet shop man said, 'Let me make you very well aware,
That Johnny Depp once owned him, so I've heard.'

OCTAVIUS THE OCTOPUS

Octavius the octopus
Has a finger in every pie.
He's my favourite at the aquarium,
I cannot pass him by.

Dexterity appeals to me –
I lack coordination.
His eight limbs move so skilfully
When they're in operation.

I wish I had eight arms like him,
I'd rather that than wings!
I'd scratch my head and pick my nose
While doing other things!

He also changes colour
And can blend with any scene.
He turns himself invisible –
On that skill I'd be keen!

There's one more thing Octavius
Can also demonstrate;
He has his own jet engine –
Now I think that would be great!

I wonder if Octavius
Knows what a whiz he is?
I feel quite armless by his side,
His skills are just the biz!

PERCY THE PORTLY PERSIAN

Percy the portly Persian
Is a bloated and ungainly version
Of a creature you might call a cat
Though some may be doubtful of that!

His fur is a terrible tangle,
His tail sticks out at an angle.
Quite filthy from nostril to tip –
He really belongs in a skip!

Percy the portly Persian
Needs a bath (I mean total immersion.)
There are so many things in his fur
That his outline is starting to blur.

His breath I'm afraid, is atrocious
And the gas from his gut is ferocious!
He's got ticks, he's got flies, he's got fleas
And he stinks like the worst kind of cheese!

Percy the portly Persian
Never manages any exertion.
He is stuck to a sticky brown mat –
I suggest you don't go touching that!!

His food is put right by his head,
So he never goes far from his bed.
When he needs to he poops in a tray
Which is only a whisker away.

Percy the portly Persian
To all travel has had an aversion.
He likes to conduct all his biz
From one place so he stays where he is!

DO NOT SNOG YOUR DOG!

Do not snog your dog,
You might as well a hog!
He slurps up lots of filthy things
And here's a catalogue:

He'll clean up all left over food,
(The mouldier the better)
He'll suck up any spillage –
Even lick it from your sweater!

He'll eat a pile of fluff, some coal,
A toe nail, sock or shoe.
He'll maul a bone, a stick, a stone,
Drink water from the loo!

He'll nibble rotting autumn leaves,
A crunchy, creepy crawly.
He'll swallow worms, dead mice,
Dead birds without becoming poorly!

Now things are getting really grim,
(Beware, I'm warning you)
You're cuddly, fluffy doggie,
Yes, he loves a piece of poo!

That friendly, dribbly, kissy pal
Who loves to lick your chops,
Likes nothing more than gobbling up
Some other doggie's plops!

So let me make it very clear
(It's not so hard to see)
That if you want to snog your dog,

FORGET IT!

LEAVE HIM BE!!

BULLDOG

I met a wide-eyed bulldog,
His eye balls bulged at me.
He sniffed and licked his floppy lips
(I think he'd just had tea.)

We stood, unsure of what to do,
We met each other's gaze.
One of us must make a move
Or we'll be here for days!

The bulldog blinked and gulped a bit,
I saw him flex a claw,
I wondered just how sharp it was
As it squeaked on the floor.

A forward step could be my last,
The bulldog thought the same,
And so with backward glances
We went back the way we came.

LABRADOODLE

That's a labradoodle,
A lab crossed with a poodle,
Or is it a doodledor?
I'm not sure anymore!

It could be a chug or a crustie
(My judgement is not very trusty)
Or maybe a cockinese –
Quite possibly any of these.

When it comes to a peekapoo,
Well I don't know, do you?
But a mongrel it's definitely not –
I'd know it at once, like a shot!

A KNOTTY PROBLEM

My dog's a knotty problem
But she doesn't care,
It doesn't mean a thing to her
That she has messy hair.

She loves a fuss and cuddles up
But when I get the comb,
She leaps up like a scalded cat
And runs away from home.

I've tried to brush her gently,
Quite softly and with care
But up she jumps and scarpers
If I snag a single hair.

I know she doesn't trust me,
She eyes me with suspicion
But she's expecting far too much,
I'm not a hair technician!

Sometimes I get her soft as silk,
I've teased out all the tangles.
She looks the perfect Afghan hound;
No hairballs, twigs or dangles!

But then she'll get out through the hedge
To spend the day in brambles,
And when she comes home for her tea
She looks a total shambles.

How could you undo all my work?
I'd pulled out every burr!
She howls as I extract a tree branch
Threaded through her fur.

You're not an Afghan any more,
You look a proper noodle.
I'll have to trim these knotted bits,
You'll end up like poodle!

BIRD WATCHING DOG

It's a terrible curse for the bird watching nut
When followed relentlessly by an old mutt.
With tongue lolling, ears flapping, prancing about,
You'll be lucky if even a chicken comes out.

You can't let him see you; he's got nowt to do
But wait to accompany someone like you!
He's a noisy annoyance, a jolloping jinx!
As an ornithological buddy he stinks.

He'll flush out a partridge, pester a duck,
Splatter your trousers with soaking wet muck.
He'll startle a blackbird, anger a wren,
Make cattle stampede, sheep jump from their pen.

He'll bark at a pheasant, at curlews he'll howl,
He'll grub out a skylark, growl at an owl.
He's a gundog supposedly (cautious and clever?)
But I don't think he's been taught anything, ever!

A bull in a china shop sums him up right,
You won't see a dicky-bird, they all take flight.
So just when I'm reaching the end of my tether,
I shin up a willow (can't do that together!)

Then shortly along comes my panting pursuit
But he's hasn't the brain box to rumble my route.
Backwards and forwards he goes looking glum
While I'm in the branches above, keeping mum.

So, always remember when plagued by a pup;
You can hide up a tree 'cos dogs never look up!
The last thing a twitcher needs (other than fog)
Is a lolloping, doolally bird watching dog!

NO ROOM AT THE BACK

Dad, there's no room at the back!
This car is unsuitably packed.
The dog's in my face
And the top of this case
Is beginning to open a crack.

Dad, there's no room in this car,
It's just not designed to go far.
You want it to race
But there's not enough space,
I wanted to bring my guitar!

Dad, the dog has a tick
And the movement is making me sick.
My Sister is grumpy,
The seating is lumpy,
Dad, stop the car, make it quick!

Dad, can you not overtake?
I'm strangled each time that you brake!
The dog's breath is smelly,
I want to watch telly,
This holiday is a mistake!

Dad, now we've got to Kings Lynne,
The novelty is wearing thin.
This tent is too small,
There's no room at all,
We're stuffed like sardines in a tin!

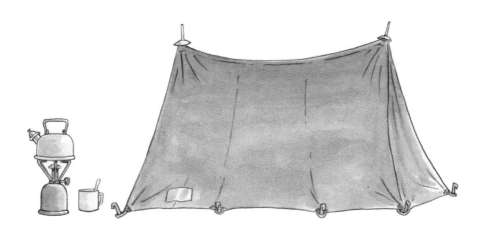

THE CROCODILE

A crocodile
It cannot smile,
It cannot suck on chips.
It cannot blow a raspberry,
The poor thing has no lips.

It cannot form an embouchure,
It cannot toot a trumpet.
It has no pout to blast it out,
No kisser fit to pump it!

So, if you meet a crocodile
And it looks sad (dejected)
A gift of brass or woodwind would
Be instantly rejected.

SCRITCH
SCRATCH

WELCOME TO MY ZOO

I WISH I HAD AN ELEPHANT

I wish I had an elephant
Or even just a lion cub
But Mum would moan and Dad would rant,
'No pets! Just join a wildlife club!'

I'd dearly love a killer whale –
No fountain needed with his spout
But our small pond is looking stale –
Dad really ought to clean it out!

A panda might be what I need
(They've got some there in London Zoo)
But they're an awkward beast to feed –
Where can I get fresh bamboo?

So, what about a kangaroo?
A giant rodent –that makes sense!
A mummy with a joey too!
But they'd jump over our back fence.

Perhaps a chimp would be quite nice?
No, Mum hates them, she thinks they're mad.
I really need some good advice,
It's ugly when an ape turns bad!

Perhaps I'm thinking much too big.
Giraffes I'd like but they're too tall.
I'll ask her for a guinea pig!
I guess all zoos have started small?

STICK INSECTS

What wonderful creatures the stick insects are!
They use camo', they don't run away.
They like to pretend that they're old broken twigs –
I could stare at their antics all day!

They can stay stock still – that would make me quite ill!
Do their joints stiffen up where they bend?
Do they muse that this ruse could mean they cannot move
When arthritis sets in the end?

DO WE HAVE TO EAT THE TURKEY?

Do we have to eat the turkey?
She is so very sweet.
She looks so keen and perky
And appears to be upbeat.

She doesn't have the faintest clue,
That she is on the menu.
For her I think the local zoo
Would be a safer venue!

She comes to me, I hold her tight
and stroke her scaly face.
She yields herself without a fight –
It's such an awkward case.

We cannot eat the turkey,
We are the folk she trusts!
She may be rather quirky
But I'd rather live on crusts!

LAWRENCE THE HOUSE MOUSE

Lawrence is a house mouse,
He loves a grand design.
He loves rococo twiddly bits,
He has a sense of line.

He'll sit in rapt attention
When antiques are on the telly.
Art nouveau or Gothic style
Just turn his legs to jelly!

I knew he loved the finer things
And vowed to help him out;
I sneaked into my Sister's room
When no one was about.

Her doll's house had all kinds of stuff
That Lawrence would adore;
Some Queen Anne chairs, a tea set,
Persian carpets for the floor.

In time, Lawrence's mouse cage
Had become completely furnished.
He spent his days French polishing
And getting brass things burnished.

Quite soon my Sister rumbled us
And after some debate,
I put back all the doll's house stuff,
I dared not hesitate!

But we had a solution to
Poor Lawrence's despair;
He moved into the doll's house
And is very happy there!

TOP GEAR HAMSTER
(A Tragedy)

I had a lovely hamster
But not for very long
His short life was a tragedy,
I'll tell you what went wrong.

I ushered him into his cage,
He ran straight to his wheel.
He jumped inside, began to ride
(He didn't want a meal.)

He whizzed around and would not cease,
I thought, is he quite right?
I lay in bed and wished for grease
(That wheel squeaked through the night.)

When morning came he still revolved.
I said, 'This cannot be!'
I weighed things up and then resolved
To set my hamster free.

I let him spin for two more days.
I thought, he needs some space.
He thinks he's running far away
While staying in one place.

But what was this? The wheel had stopped!
An eerie silence where
My friend lay prone upon his back
With four feet in the air!

My hamster could have won a race!
At top speed he'd been spinning
But if you just rotate in space,
You've got no chance of winning.

I think at first, he did not know
That he would go nowhere.
I guess in time he thought it through
And clapped out in despair!

VANILLA CHINCHILLA

My chinchilla likes vanilla,
She likes mint and chocolate chip.
Her hutch is like a villa
But she doesn't think it's hip.

She loves a bag of roasted nuts
And cherry flavoured fudge.
It may be why, when bedtime comes,
She's not prepared to budge.

She grips the carpet with her claws
And makes an angry sound.
She shuns her posh, expensive hutch –
She wants to stick around.

She'll hide beneath the largest chair,
She'll sneak behind a curtain.
We all forget that she's inside –
She's in her hutch for certain!

Now no one wants to go outside
Where it is cold and dark.
Chinchilla knows that's how we feel
So, stealthily she'll park.

When, in the morning, we come down
And through the lounge all troop,
We slip and slide on mystery crumbs
Mixed with chinchilla poop.

And there she is upon a chair
Like Lady Lah-di-dah.
She's polished off a bowl of fruit
And a jumbo chocolate bar!

HERBERT THE TORTOISE
(Another tragedy)

Herbert is a tortoise,
Courageous, brave and bold.
He looks wrinkly and ancient
But he isn't very old.

If you just wave a lettuce
He is on you like a cheetah –
Admittedly a sluggish one,
But just as keen an eater.

He stamps his chunky little legs
And stretches forth his neck.
His claws screech on the paving slabs
When he comes for a peck.

He loves a varied crop of greens,
He yanks them from the dirt.
He reaches up for runner beans
And sometimes chews my shirt.

Oh Herbert, what a plucky chap
You really seem to be,
Chomping up all kinds of stuff
If you can tear it free.

So why did you, dear Herbert,
Clap out in hibernation?
We thought your tea chest packed with straw
Was warm incarceration?

Now, forever in your shell,
However loud I shout,
I know that scaly little head
Is never popping out.

No more will you stride through the daisies
Ambling like the clappers,
Towards some brightly coloured blooms
That are in fact, sweet wrappers.

COLLIE WOBBLES

Our collie is a healthy dog,
His fur flows like a river
But when he's eaten something odd
His tummy starts to quiver.

He pants and coughs and rolls his eyes
And dribbles like a tap.
His padding paws pace up and down
As if he's in a trap!

I want to ease his grumbly-tum'
And make his panic pass
But he knows doggie medicine
And scoffs a bunch of grass.

He hacks and heaves as if near death
Then writhes upon the floor.
He's making me feel queasy now,
We need a vet for sure!

Then suddenly he's prancing,
Bright and jolly on the cobbles.
Our collie has bounced back again
From the awful collie wobbles.

Jelly Terror!
(A horror story)

Jellyfish are everywhere,
They stretch across the beach
And so, for my soft naked feet,
The sea is out of reach.

And thus it is for many folk
Who must avoid the error
Of stepping on the frightful blob
That is the jelly terror!

You see, the seaside is so great,
A perfect place to play.
It's unfair that those scary blobs
Get in a persons way.

It's really just as though those monsters
Know that we're about
And heap themselves upon our beach
Instead of spreading out!

They may be harmless, who can tell?
Our parents do not know.
They just say, 'Best not touch them,
You can keep on tippy-toe.'

Dad said that he once knew a boy
Who got stung on the thigh.
It swelled to almost twice its size
And nearly made him die!

I tripped one day while trotting by
A very massive blobber.
My foot went slap right on its cap –
It squished out goo and slobber!

I screamed as if the end had come –
They'd got me, those big jellies!
And so, to combat jelly terror
Now I wear my wellies!

BEING A PUPPY
(A true story)

'Darling what have you been doing?
Your face is all covered in cream!'
'I'm being a puppy,' I said, feeling proud.
Mummy let out a very loud scream!

SCOTTIE
(A wee bit of advice)

Hoo to handle a Scottie
(Ye ruffians please tak' heed)
Doon't hoist 'im up bi the bottie,
Doon't hang 'im high bi th' lead!

Doon't fret that yon doogie might tangle,
He'll tamp back doon ye will see.
Doon't bi th' throat let 'im dangle,
Let Scotties gae wild an' free!

71

CREEPY CRAWLIES

Creepy crawlies know what tall is,
They'd be tall instead of smallies.
Fleas don't like to be so titchy,
They get squished when we get itchy.

Worms and slugs get splattered flat,
Snails go crunch – imagine that!
Spiders tumble down the loo –
No life raft just a floating poo!

Woodlice dread the vacuum cleaner,
Butterflies wish things were greener.
Bees say, 'please, not toxic vapour!'
Flies despise a rolled up paper.

Worms just squirm when on a hook,
Gnats get flattened by a book.
Silver fish have one last wish;
To be enormous and then – SQUISH!

Creepy crawlies they despise none,
They are folk who have no flies on.
So, just watch those clumsy feet
Or creepy crawlies are dead meat!

SEA HORSES

When you see sea horses,
You see horses in the sea,
At least, you think they're horses
But strange fish is what they be.

They don't let people ride them
And they don't take part in races,
It just so happens that they have
Such horsey looking faces.

So if you see a sea horse,
Of course it may well be
That it is just a proper horse
That likes it in the sea.

RODNEY THE RHINO

Rodney was a rhino
Who roamed the ragged plain.
He'd trot down to the water-hole
And then trot back again.

He loved to crush a lonely shrub
When stamping through the bush;
He'd trample it to bits and pieces
Turning it to mush.

One day Molly Meercat said,
'What do you do that for?
Beating down that lovely shrub
That's just outside my door!'

Rodney hung his heavy head
And said, 'I don't know really.
I didn't think, I didn't know
That you might love it dearly.'

'Well so I do,' said Molly
With her paws upon her hips,
'But now my little flowering shrub
Is mashed up into chips!'

'Go and find another shrub
And dig it up for me,
Then plant it here beside my door
And tread more carefully!'

So Rodney did what Molly said
And things were all put right.
He saw that busting things for fun
Is really not too bright.

MRS FLOSSY COTTON BOTTOM

Mrs Flossy Cotton Bottom
Asked me round for tea
But dandelions and thistle down
Are not the food for me.

'Oh do partake of toadstool pie
And have some teasel tart.'
Dear Mrs Flossy Cotton Bottom,
I must now depart.

'But blue bell batch and cicely greens
You surely can't refuse?'
Oh Mrs Flossy Cotton
I would rather eat my shoes!

My colon cannot cope with food
That rabbits can digest.
So Mrs Flossy Cotton Bottom,
Fare thee well, 'tis best.

NOISY BADGER

I met a noisy badger
One bright and moonlit night,
Crashing through the undergrowth
But I soon put him right.

I said, 'Why not be careful
When you are on the move?'
He said, 'I care not whether you
Of my technique approve.'

'I stamp and champ and stomp and chomp
And rummage gleefully.
I do not need advice
From stealthy slinkers such as thee!'

So there I left the badger
Creating such a sound
That many creatures shook their heads
And ran back underground.

You see, I like to travel
With a soft and silent tread.
An awful din is just the thing
Us clever foxes dread!'

THE FERRET AND THE WEASEL

A ferret met a weasel –
They faced up eye to eye.
Weasel said to Ferret,
'You're a larger size than I.'

Ferret said to Weasel,
'Yes that certainly is true
But who has sharper gnashers –
Is it me or is it you?'

Weasel said, 'Who gets down holes
And never in a jam?'
Ferret said, 'You're very skinny –
More so than I am.'

So Ferret and the Weasel,
Although not quite the same,
Agreed to work together
At the rabbit catching game.

Their venture was successful
And their bellies grew so round
That in the end not one nor t'other
Could get underground.

So Ferret and the Weasel
Shook paws and said goodbye.
''Twas lovely while it lasted
But we're too good, you and I.'

I'VE GOT CRABS

I've got crabs, do you want to see?
This one's Bruce and this one's Lee.
They look like great big flat meat pies.
They've got eight legs and googly eyes.

I wish I had their grabby grippers,
Just like Grandad's garden clippers!
I'd like to take them home you see
But Mum says,

'DON'T BRING THEM NEAR ME!!'

AARDVARK

I thought I saw an aardvark
Trotting past a tree –
Running through the car park
At twenty five to three!

I thought. Am I mistaken?
Could such things be about?
But what else has those rabbit ears
And such a big long snout?

What other creature has those claws
And little twinkly eyes?
To see an aardvark in a car park –
What a nice surprise!

GOLDFISH

I won a goldfish at a fair
But it wasn't fair.
I had nowhere
To put my fish.
I used a dish.
The fish went splish.
It needed a shoal
Not a breakfast bowl.
I stared into its eyes unblinking –
My heart sinking
I didn't know what it was thinking.

The fish looked tired
And then expired,
Probably because I fed it a marsh mallow
And the dish was too shallow –
A bit like the bloke at the fair
Who cheerfully handed out goldfish to children
Without bothering to find out
Whether they were experienced in
Caring for captive marine animals!

SAUSAGE DOG

I know a little sausage dog
Whose legs are short and stumpy.
His tubby tummy tickles
If the road he's on is lumpy.

Dotty, trotty sausage dog
Likes keeping very busy.
He doesn't like to be up high,
It always makes him dizzy.

Oh, how I love that sausage dog
Though very low he be.
He may be only one foot high
But long-ways two foot three!

I HAD A LITTLE PONY

I had a little pony, I had him for a while
But then his sweet-some temperament turned rapidly to bile.
He kicked me up the underpants, he hoofed me in the head.
That cuddly looking bronco had me totally misled!

I gave him one more season, I gave him one more try.
I said to him, 'You must behave' and he spat in my eye.
He dragged me through the branches,
He spun me round and round,
He shot me up into the air and dashed me to the ground.

I found him hiding in a wood with other naughty creatures,
Peeping from an ivy bush but I discerned his features.
I said, 'right, that's it now, you're far too wild for me!
The hospital have told me that I have to set you free.'

RAMBLING BEAST

I chanced upon a rambling beast
That foxed my keenest eye.
I spied it through an unkempt hedge.
I gasped and said, Oh my!

What kind of beast might this one be?
A yak, an ape, a moose?
Perhaps a woolly mammoth now
Is back and on the loose?

A frizzy, fuzzy, hairy lump
With neither end confirmed.
I twiddled my binoculars –
How could this thing be termed?

Then the creature tossed its head,
Through yellow teeth it squealed.
A pony like a haystack
Was quite suddenly revealed.

My goodness me, I was surprised
About that fluffy clump.
It's quite a shock when you can't tell
The head end from the rump!

Parents;

If you and your children have enjoyed this book, please tell me what you thought of it. Just look up the book again where you purchased it and find the bit where you can write a review, and remember, be kind to all small beasts and even kinder to the big ones that might accidentally tread on your foot if you frighten them.

Mark Bardsley

Here are some secret pages to use
for your own animal poems!

I always write in pencil when I am composing a poem, that way I
can rub stuff out if it isn't working. Another thing I always do is
read my poems out loud to myself. If your poem sounds good and
flows well when you read it, that's a good sign that you've written
a great poem!
I've put some illustrations at the bottom of each writing page
which I hope will give you some ideas.

The "Dog's" Bog

"Why, there's a dog in a bog!"
"What shall I do?"

37077649R00057

Printed in Great Britain
by Amazon